YOGA CATS™

ℛ
RAVETTE PUBLISHING

First published by Ravette Publishing 2011
Reprinted in 2011, 2014, 2015

Ravette Publishing Limited
PO Box 876
Horsham
West Sussex RH12 9GH

ISBN: 978-1-84161-356-7

Let's
do
Yoga

I can, can...

Can you can, can?

FRANKLIN
Heron Pose
(Krounchasana)

Cat-ch!

EVA
Eagle Pose
(Garudasana)

YOGA

ANYONE?

Whatever makes

you feel good

GHOST
Feathered
Peacock Pose
(Pincha Mayurasana)

We all have

our hang-ups!

PERSIA

Sleeping Vishnu Pose
(Anantasana)

Purr ... fectly

Balanced

SNOOSH
Handstand
(Adho Mukha
Vrksasana)

Let your Paws

lead

the way

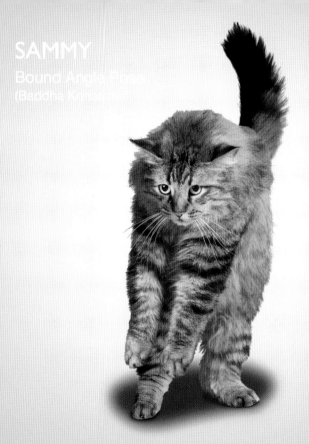

SAMMY

Bound Angle Pose
(Baddha Konasana)

Say a little

prayer for me

MING

Mountain Pose
(Tadasana)

What me ...

rollover?

BOLILLO

Corpse Pose
(Savasana)

Sit and stay
in the
moment

SNOWSHOES

Open - Angle Seated Pose
(Uphavista Konasana)

IT'S A

CAT-ASTROPHE!

I don't
do
ordinary!

MAUDE

Side Plank Pose
(Adho Mukha Svanasana)

I do it

my way

SNOWSHOES BABY

Happy Baby Pose
(Ananda Balasana)

Feline

Groovy

STAR

Triangle Pose
(Utthita Trikonasana)

Other titles available in this series ...

		ISBN	Price
Animal Yoga	**(new)**	978-1-84161-390-1	£5.99
Cow Yoga	**(new)**	978-1-84161-389-5	£5.99
Yoga Babies		978-1-84161-377-2	£4.99
Yoga Dogs - Get in Touch With Your Inner Pup		978-1-84161-357-4	£4.99
Yoga Kittens - Take Life One Pose at a Time		978-1-84161-362-8	£4.99
Yoga Puppies - The Ruff Guide to Yoga		978-1-84161-363-5	£4.99

How to order   Please send a cheque/postal order in £ sterling, made payable
to 'Ravette Publishing' for the cover price of books and
allow the following for post & packaging ...

UK & BFPO	70p for the first book & 40p per book thereafter
Europe and Eire	£1.30 for the first book & 70p per book thereafter
Rest of the world	£2.20 for the first book & £1.10 per book thereafter

RAVETTE PUBLISHING LTD
PO Box 876, Horsham, West Sussex RH12 9GH
Tel: 01403 711443   Fax: 01403 711554   Email: info@ravettepub.co.uk
www.ravettepublishing.tel

Prices and availability are subject to change without prior notice.